LIGHT THROUGH WATER
CONNOR COGILL

This is a work of fiction. All names, characters, places, and incidents are a product of the author's imagination. Any resemblance to real events or persons, living or dead, is entirely coincidental.

Published by Akashic Books
©2024 Connor Cogill
ISBN: 978-1-63614-221-0

All rights reserved
Printed in China
First printing

Akashic Books
Instagram, X, Facebook: AkashicBooks
info@akashicbooks.com
www.akashicbooks.com

African Poetry Book Fund
Prairie Schooner
University of Nebraska
110 Andrews Hall
Lincoln, Nebraska 68588

TABLE OF CONTENTS

Preface by Uhuru Phalafala 5

Continent without a name 9
Light through water 11
In search of warmth 13
Underripe 14
I wait in avocados 16
List of least graceful things 17
Sunday roast 18
Men in water 20
Tantalus 21
Cyborg in swimming pool 23
Fruit salad 25
Footsteps recede 26
I don't know what I'm praying to 28
December 29
Where clouds gather 30
To save a country 31
Cryptid 32
Revisionist history 33

Acknowledgments 34

PREFACE
by Uhuru Phalafala

To those for whom history has played out intimately in and on their bodies, history is deeply felt—it courses through their veins. In South African writer Connor Cogill's lush poetry in *Light Through Water*, "time is just a deep pool / that bends us." The questions he asks express an embodied history bent by time: can he stay calm, control his breathing, and make himself light? Can he be weightless? Locating history in the body renders history a breathing, sensuous, eruptive, and visceral thing.

When time is a refracted light through these pooled, inscrutable waters, the poetics of bending are generated aplenty. There is the matter of the son whose great-great-great-grandfather fought in a war, and the grandson's questions that are never asked: *whose war*? And more pertinent still, *whose land* is the family home on? This history is evinced in "century-old family portraits which / hang lopsided in the family home." ("Continent without a name")

Cogill's poetry lives in the warped passage of time; for him, wars not only "hang on the wall[s]" but also "flow through / [his] veins." ("Continent without a name") War is thrust upon him in the present, too, through romantic relationships: "I am fruit picked fresh / and split straight down the middle." ("Underripe") Later, he lays claim to mother as origin and car as capital city, as country of birth, as continent. He derives meaning from refracting in the deep pool of time, from his birth in the back seat of a car to his grandmother's death, unmarked by a headstone. In aligning these two monuments in his family lineage—of grandmother, mother, and himself in rites of passages of birth and death—Cogill sings matrilineal belonging and becoming. He queers patrilineal identification through troubling the terrains of "ancestors ... buried in the family plot," of a "lineage [that] is exact." In his view, the unasked and unaskeable questions about the wars, land, and women in his lineage, make the otherwise heroic, century-old family narrative skew. ("Continent without a name") He is revising his history.

In his revisionary poetry, he writes about his mother's late brother, who used to wear her lipstick:

> Because in some version of history I am
> the dead uncle, my life a question
> unanswered.
> ("Revisionist history")

The poet explores his sexuality and its imbrication with patriarchal past-presents of the family, race, heteronormativity, and queer violence. In a South Africa troubled by the afterlives of conflict and land grabs, "kindness alone will not be the shape / of revolution." ("Where clouds gather") The question that sits breathing in every poem, in every line, is—can he make himself light in this deep pool of time? For he "re-member[s his] wiring, / the crushing mechanical comfort / of human cosplay." ("Cyborg in swimming pool") As a queer male of this heritage, this nation, this land, and this family, the poet's critical consciousness bends at a deeper level.

We sense distress that is commonplace in excavating lineage; plunging into these waters brings history and politics to the surface. Their interplay causes havoc—"I down my drink and half drown / in the swimming pool" ("In search of warmth")—and a yearning for love. This quest makes space for beauty as Cogill's narrative deftly subverts the heroics of history and its patrimonial aesthetics by centering sensuality and the erotic; even the veins of his hands are years that have passed, "heaving roots beneath [his] skin." ("Sunday roast")

We are reminded here that the past has not passed, that history lives in the present and can devour us, our warm bodies ripe and heavy like fruit. ("To save a country") His body is devoured not only by lovers, but by the land itself, functioning as an offering to this contested and political space. The land stains his body like mulberries, "spilling black into the dirt and foliage." ("To save a country") To be claimed by the land in South Africa, even as one with complicated lineage, queers an understanding of being and belonging beyond the ownership paradigm of great-great-great-grandfathers, of patriarchs. It is a small riot. It is an intervention at a bodily level that recasts the land as far older and deeper than any human life and logic, that surrenders to the wildness of the winds and trees, the cycles of seasons and fruit, the oceans that hold centuries and millennia "which stare [him] into submission." ("Where clouds gather") It is a thing of beauty to be able to explore and grapple with other forms of belonging here in this country today; we welcome Connor Cogill's meditations to the larger corpus of contemporary African poetry.

CONTINENT WITHOUT A NAME

Today, as we flit past
the graveyard on our way home, I see
the gray headstones dyed canary yellow
by sunset and think of the grandmother
whom I have never met, my father's mother,
who stands poised in grayscale on the wall,
and warm in Father's memories. I think how
lucky you are, whose ancestors are buried
in the family plot. You whose lineage is
exact, century-old family portraits, which
hang lopsided in the family home. Say, This
is my great-great-great-grandfather, who
fought in a war. Say, This home has been
in our family for generations. I will not ask
whose war. I will not ask whose land. I will
tell a charming story: how I was born in
the backseat of a car because the nurses
didn't know shit and sent my bursting mother
home. This car seat I bless, call my capital,
my country. These polyesters, my hospital.
Mother's fingers, the midwife, guiding me
from womb to winter, the cold of August
night, which blew heavy at the window.
And as I think this, the graveyard passing
in a yolky ribbon of color, I recall how
Grandma has no headstone, no one place to
mark her resting bones, or highlight golden
at dusk, or leave carnations. How she
worked her fingers rough but

could not afford the final chunk of stone.
Photograph in lieu of headstone. My parents,
station wagon in lieu of hospital plan. I ask
if you know what it means, you whose wars
hang on the wall rather than flow through
your veins, to call a car your continent
or be buried without a name.

LIGHT THROUGH WATER

Now here, in this
perfect pool, so new still

that the surrounding earth
has not set—there is you, five,
maybe six, learning to swim.

You cling to the edges, to
bricks just planted,
palms pressed firmly
to the frail illusion of safety.

Then, a voice. Mom's hand
on your back. *Stay calm.*
Control your breathing.
Make yourself light.
Here, laid flat, you are

a leaf on the water.

Open your eyes.
Have you ever seen anything
quite this blue? Now turn,
now paddle. Yes, stay light.

Now, at the edge of this
leaking pool, you nurse a bottle.

I keep thinking about light

refracted through water.
How time is just a deep pool
that bends us. Have we
done it yet? Are we weightless?

IN SEARCH OF WARMTH

I face an army of geckos today,
the warmest day since forever ago;

they stand on guard, scattered
across the lawn, on lookout on
the wall, perched on a pile of dogshit.

Legion of eyes at once blinking
as I down my drink and half drown
in the swimming pool

then crawl toward the bricks
in search of warmth or
whatever is to be found in this,

which keeps the lizards returning
even now as they poke their heads out
from the mint bush,

split tongues brandished,
risking the giant for a piece of sun.

UNDERRIPE

This evening I go to a wedding, watch
in awe, then cry in the bathroom.
There are poems on my tongue as I try
to contain them; I do not let them go

until the morning when it is you
again on my doorstep. I want
to bathe you and keep you,
but you will not be held, only
swallowed and spat back out
like food from the crow's mouth.

I lie naked and wait
for you to return as the light leaks
brighter through the curtains, spills
over the bedding
while clanging in the kitchen
you prepare coffee to bring me down

from wine pilfered off tables last night,
the wedding-goers distracted
by the bride and groom who sway
round the dance floor like willows
that sweep the water's surface;
I can only say I wish that were us.

Rather, you are a branch that shatters
my light into fragments on the pavement.
A breath and you are gone. I am

swinging alone in the living room
for the birds on the windowpane
that pick at their reflections,

and it is last night again:
me, drunk in a bathroom stall,
caging words until whenever you return
to devour me and discard me—

for you I am a fruit picked fresh
and split straight down the middle.

I WAIT IN AVOCADOS

I name them,

the men I see in the grocery store,
and for five minutes we share a love,
an apartment somewhere untouchable,
like the bird's nest in backyard ivy.

Me and Tony—that's his name—adopt
a puppy, and he lets me name her too.
Kimberly Jones sleeps cradled in my neck
between the crevices of this perfect life.

The boy shopping for potatoes is my fiancé,
the second one, but this time will work out.
For Theo, I make pasta from scratch, and he
pads across the kitchen with garlic for the sauce.

Teddy is searching for soft bread now.
I shoot him a look that says, *Meet me*
by the produce / We'll kiss in avocados / This
time the apples won't come tumbling down.

For once I will feel real.

He shoots one back that says,
Can I help you sir?

LIST OF LEAST GRACEFUL THINGS

there is dawn, a sky undone by light
to bring clear into view the birds fallen
from trees shucked as consequence, earth
pelted by amber leaves, and rain, and sun.
Sleepily, the clouds reach for it and just
barely miss us, grazing shivs of grass,
the anthill, the birdbath. We remember
mornings in lives past, sunrise soft
as flesh, buttered toast and milky tea
in plastic mugs slid across the table
by Mom. Before small sins illuminated
by daybreak and regret poured into regret
as I draw a too-hot bath. Now, the sun
threatens to carry us away. Through
another silent morning just the same,
and the husks of fruit pecked apart
by sunbirds. Still, I eat hope for breakfast,
while like a bloodied egg into a frying pan,
the day cracks open over us.

SUNDAY ROAST

At some point it was simpler, when through
my mother's eyes I could see the universe; us
beneath the moonflower tree in the yard
where peach petals bled into yellow, the sun
at a dip beneath the Vibracrete, my father
with a glass of whiskey and a cigar
as he tells a story, waving hands like branches.
This is a tiny world—only the schoolyard
and my siblings, the television and garden,
my parents and these Sunday meals.

In the story it is my father, no older than me,
as he gets into a fight on the way to a fair.
I can see it as I sit, my gentle willow of a father,
who then was a sapling. With these words
he sews past to present, each memory a stitch
in this quilt that leads to the future, from him
to my mother, to the me of then and now.
Still this is simple, the sun setting over us
as we laugh and I stare at my hands, tracing
the veins of them

until the years have passed,
and they have lifted like my father's, now
heaving roots beneath my skin. We sit
around the plastic dining table, those of us left
gathered for a Sunday roast, while my father
recounts the same story as though it is new,
and again we laugh—though knowing

it is less simple this time, the quilt
no longer ending here; stitches stretched
in each direction, to my brother across country
and my sister at her new job, to the freckled
hands of my father,

who finishes the story with a half smile
then cuts into his meal in silence.
It ends here: Sunday lunch
beneath the moonflower tree,
which now withers.

MEN IN WATER

We are in the water, he
and I, in a swimming hole carved
into the side of the mountain, the
glistening mouth of a craggy face,
and it is soft and sweet,
the warmth of our bodies
in this cold, deep pool, legs
that brush beneath the water,
large hands laced together; we
crawl out onto the heated rocks,
shivering figures pressed closely
together, and it is all I have been
missing; this tenderness
which need not explain itself,
the mountain range in-line with
the slope of his frame, convulsing
as he tries to catch his breath,
flesh beating beneath skin
as though there is a heart
in each muscle—all this to say:

Here, this beauty reflected
through us, is the meaning
of Desire. *I am*
filled with it.

TANTALUS

I
My yearning wakes at dawn,
stares out the kitchen window and
into the hollow street

as I pretend I am the kind who could
relish a smoke or the bottle, or kind words
from a man with pure intentions. Some
guilty pleasure beyond wanting
that which I am not allowed.

Since the beginning I've craved beauty
hungered longed reached for
as the flightless bird stares at olives
overhead—Tantalus in his prison,
I'd do anything to feel right.

For now, only the trumpet
of an ambulance down the street,
rats emerging from their shitholes,
blunted steel of sunrise
withdrawn from its sheath

as the silent legion swarms to war.
I wonder if their yearning keeps score too
then imagine I have something spectacular
to say. Spectacular.
Beyond that I am hungry.

II
For beauty as in 04:16
I wake to piss and watch the streetlamp
flicker through the frosted bathroom window
and for a moment I am held, I forget
the goose chase, know nothing beyond this.

And I am not hungry anymore.
I can't even recall the feeling.

CYBORG IN SWIMMING POOL

From March to March
the months forget themselves, swim
'til they can barely float, through autumn
and August and the half slumber

of September, until we're just north
of summer and north of campus again,
forgetful on a wine farm, reacquainting
with my outside face, outside voice, outside

inhibitions—never blinking too much,
or smiling too hard, or unscrewing my grip.
Today, freedom is almost new again, something
shiny to master the controls of.

I pull down the lever too hard, almost
admit I've come to hate the taste of truth,
mostly from my own tongue.

April is just numb. I see my friends a lot.
Haunt the street. Remember my wiring,
the crushing mechanical comfort
of human cosplay.

Today is the last swim of the year. Winter
waits overhead. I want to be someone who
has mastered both sincerity and shamelessness,
though I fear they are as dreams to forgetting.

Another birthday and the water
is too cold. I'm still a liar who misremembers
how to move beyond muscle memory, beyond
just swimming.

FRUIT SALAD

I'm at the counter again
wondering where the strawberries went

as I deseed a pomegranate, bloody
and bright into a bowl of yogurt,
then lick out the husk.

It's June now and I haven't seen you in years.
Sometimes I catch a glimpse in a window
then hurry home to sing the old songs.

I know I can't keep dancing in pyramids
trying to resurrect some old body of mine,
but I miss the way the night once held you.

When I commit, I can see us still—
counting cars poured over asphalt
and bodies over bricks, gate upon gate

upon gate. And in some room, through
some mucky window, shrapnel of a silhouette
just barely remembering itself,

a knife slides through apples at dawn.
I'm on the counter again.
Who's peeling whom?

FOOTSTEPS RECEDE

In ways I am immovable.
Not the ceiling. Each morning
it inches closer, until today I wake and it is
pressed to my nose, breathing down on me

as a lover does,
and I think nothing of it
because moths have cocooned and emerged
in the time since I have last been kissed,

and he is fucking some other man he calls
His Handsome
as I teach myself new ways to make the roof
trusses seem farther away, the drinks

growing more bitter and frequent—
at midday I call from the edge of the pool,
rather, dial with my fingertips on the water, then
listen for the ring with my head in my hands;

I think maybe you'd love me more if I were taller,
or I learned to say goodbye the way you do—
you wipe your feet on the way out of my house
and that's the last of you, that's the last of you

as you cross the street and into your car.
I press my ear to the blue
and hear nothing but deep hollow
for miles and miles, your footsteps

like an insect on the water's surface,
only vibrating in the distance.

I DON'T KNOW WHAT I'M PRAYING TO

Over a toilet seat, half God, half
piss. Over lips, and feet and arms
and smalls of backs.

Over rosary beads, some safety
sketched from boyhood. Over
trampolines and Apple Munch
and necks of bottles and necks
of boys.

I don't know what I'm praying to.
Sometimes I shut my eyes mid-
dance; is this worship?
Or flashes of persimmon when I
fall asleep in the car?

God, make me a leather couch.
I'd like his handprints in my side.
God, make me a window. I'd like to know
what people happier than me think
when they look out at the street.

DECEMBER

Darkness draws shut another year
and I go in alone, heat stinging like hornets
as I sing along to that song—the one that
persuades I am not hollow if only
for a minute.

By its end I've grown tired
of addressing my shadow, granting it hands
with which to choke me. Then the fireworks.
You share a kiss with someone else, no doubt.
While I share a glance with my reflection,

who understands best the mechanics
of my bullshit. That I'm tired of love
through a window. Somewhere tonight
you'll remember me then forget
like a New Year's resolution.

For now, the sky is bright as poison.

WHERE CLOUDS GATHER

Once my city meant lights,
a sticker book come to life as we
crept through its center bright with Christmas
and the yellows of samosas Father to this day
insists on buying each time we cross them.
I imagine the smells are a whisper to his past
as those night markets are to mine.
Or winding Hout Bay round and through
until the water below is a jade too particular
to capture beyond the eyes of memory,

which stare me into submission now.
I am as a dog at supper waiting to be fed
by a city that has changed less so in history
and more so in meaning I can no longer simplify.
I know that kindness alone will not be the shape
of revolution. I know I still love the beach and
the pomegranate of sunset, that most things
are sweeter before understanding. Cape Town
is named for its wind, is named for its fury
I cannot unhear

even as I turn from it.

TO SAVE A COUNTRY

One summer there was a mulberry tree
that sprouted suddenly in the backyard heavy
with fruit spilling black into the dirt and foliage.
I sat and gorged myself in the cool shadowy corner
until my hands were purple, until summer left
and with it took the mulberry tree, shriveled
to nothing but stains of its sweet dark bearings.

One summer I read a book
about a little boy lost in North America,
and I wondered if I was like him, only in Africa—
I have a bad habit of making things about myself,
even now as the Cape Town wind bays (as it does)
and I convince myself that it's me it is reviling, me
the center of all things, the one with the purple hands.

This summer swallows us whole.
I wonder what else is to be found here.
Besides houses which are merely windows
or once-tree patches of earth. I shut my eyes, run
my fingers over the blank space.
Questions stain my hands. To run or to save?
Is there saving in this at all, small as I am,

the child beneath the mulberry tree?

CRYPTID

Can't stop thinking about all the faces
vanished from my life like streetlights
crashing tangerine through curtain cracks

then abandoned by dawn.

This morning I hazard tracing my gloom
to some shard of familiarity, slice an orange
ten pieces too many.

I'm forgetting your eyes and the orbit
of your gait. By midday I've forgotten
I wished to remember at all.

Strange faces fixed to stranger
bodies, or some version of history
holding us in craters.

REVISIONIST HISTORY

There are wounds I do not press,
like the question of my dead uncles.
My mother only tells me her brother
liked to play with her lipstick sometimes;
I wonder if in her gentle way there is something
she is trying to say. My father only tells me
his brother loved spanspek split in half
and devoured straight out the rind—
I imagine that's how you would eat the sun.
I do not ask anything more not only
because I am selfless
but because I am selfish, because I do not want
to know which doors have been shut to me.
Because in some version of history I am
the dead uncle, my life a question
unanswered.

ACKNOWLEDGMENTS

Acknowledgment and thanks to the following publications and journals, where some of these poems found their first homes:

New Contrast: "Sunday roast"

Johannesburg Review of Books: "Light through water" and "List of least graceful things"

The Sol Plaatje European Union Poetry Anthology: "To save a country"

Jack Journal: "Continent without a name"

The poems "Continent without a name" and "Revisionist history" were shortlisted for the Brunel International African Poetry Prize and appeared on the *African Poetry Prize* website in this capacity.